LONG STORY SHORT

AN ANTHOLOGY OF 20 SHORT STORIES

SHRUTI

To my 13 year old self,

Who dreamt of writing a book.

Contents

Acknowledgements

I have to start by thanking my mother for listening to my short stories and talking round me into publishing an anthology. Forever grateful for the coolest mumma I've gotten. And to my sister for always listening to the stories I've written wholeheartedly.

Also, Jiya for always being there to guide me and giving me the best possible advice for my book. Last but definitely not the least, my best friend Daksha for being so fascinated by my stories and for giving me the amazing reviews that kept me going. I'm so happy that these people exist!!!

I

SHE DID IT

1.

She Did It

Hey I'm Betty, a 14 y/o girl. I used to be a topper in my class. But ever since my mother died, I have failed in every subject. Worse came to the worst and my father remarried. And guess what? My step-mother turned out to be absolutely wicked, like any other fairytale step mom.

She always abuses me for failing exams. Though, she is the reason I've been failing every subject. The only human I like in the world is Mary, my best friend. We are besties ever since I can remember. I remember playing Freeze tag with my mother and Mary when we were small. My mother loved both of us the same. It was a spellbinding bond.... Until my mother died and I was forced to live in the same house with my step mom.

Now, my mother had left the world but I got Mary by my side. I was done, with my step-mom and her taunts. So, I decided to ace in the upcoming exams. I worked hard and was confident of my marks for the tests. I didn't just want to get good grades, I wanted to be on the top, only to put an end to my step-mom's harrasment.

My results were out. I got good grades. I excelled. But wasn't on the top though. I was disappointed to see some girl named Tina above me.

Some girl Tina beat me.

And yes, my step-mom wasn't pleased to see my results either. Even though I was the second best, my step-mom had a marvelous time insulting me.

The next day in school, I chewed the back of my pen, and took Tina to the girl's washroom. Few days later, our teacher announced that Tina's hands were severely injured and her parents had decided to take Tina away from the school. Tina never came back. I was happy. I could ace the tests since some girl Tina was gone.

Months passed, and the results for the Final examinations were about to come out. I was more than certain that I would ace the class, since that Tina was gone.

Turned out, I was the second best yet again, and below my best friend Mary.

I hadn't aced the exams, Mary did.

I glared at Mary's hand, chewed the back of my pen, and said-

"Mary, let's get you inside the washroom."

~written by a blood-smeared pen.

II

BETTY (SHE DID IT PT. 2)

2.

Betty

Ryan was packing boxes after boxes of clothes and all the other stuff he would necessarily need since he was moving out with his family.

He realised that living there in the house where his daughter Betty had spent her entire childhood was becoming tough, since her mother was no longer with her.

He thought his second marriage would make it better for his daughter but it only did her worse.

A Lot of bad things had happened to his daughter in the past year. Betty's mother had died, her best friend Mary had gotten her hand severely injured in the school washroom and had to be taken away for better treatment. She hadn't talked to her since then. They later found out that Mary had died shortly after that incident. Betty hadn't smiled ever since those things had happened.

It was tough for Ryan to see his daughter that way and moving out of the house with millions of her mother's and Mary's memories seemed the best thing to do for her.

Betty was out in the garden. Swinging, When Ryan went into her room to box all the necessary things for her.

He picked up her photo frame, the one where she seemed happy with her mother and her best friend Mary. Probably the last time she was that happy.

Ryan kept the frame into the box. Then he picked up some drawings that she had drawn with Mary when they were small. He tossed them in as well.

The drawer had gone empty and he was done with her drawer when he realised that there was some stick attached to the drawer. He touched it and it went down. The drawer shifted and revealed a diary that was kept hidden in the secret space nobody knew the drawer had. Nobody, except Betty.

He picked the diary up. He knew it was a secret diary not meant for anyone to read. But there he was. A father. Curious. He opened it.

"I glared at Mary's hand, chewed the back of my pen and said-

"Mary, let's get you inside the washroom

~written from a blood smeared pen"

Ryan closed the diary with shaking hands. He was terrified. Of his own daughter. Did she really? Did she really kill her own best friend? Yes, she did. It was all in the diary.

She did it.

He just realised the enormity of what she did. Ryan went to the park. Not knowing what to do. Not just questioning his parenting. But questioning the existence of his own daughter.

He didn't know that his second wife abused her. Maybe he didn't know anything happening in the house at all.

Was he supposed to turn her in? Or send her to therapy? He couldn't decide what had to be done. He knew Mary was dead. And that her killer was out there, swinging in his garden. Probably thinking about what she had done. Or maybe just thinking about what she was about to do next. Ryan realised he didn't know his own daughter. At All.

He could call 911 right then and there. Or maybe he could just shut up. Because what could be the consequences of it? He realised.That he had raised a psychopath. He knew what he had to do. He wasn't going to call the police. He wasn't going to shut up either.

He went to the garden swing where Betty was sitting. Not swinging. Just traumatised enough by the loss of her best friend, the one she killed herself.

She heard something behind her. She looked behind. She saw his father behind with a plough. It smelled like compost. And everything after that was blurred. It smelled like death then.

Ryan came back into the room with his hands covered in blood. His daughter's blood.

Just like Betty's pen was. In Mary's blood.

He looked at all her things in the box. Her photographs. Her drawings. Her diary. He opened the diary again. Read the pages. Then read another few pages he was yet to read but couldn't because of what the first few had written on them.

"There was this story writing competition in my English class. That was the first class I had attended after knowing about Mary's death. I was too stunned to go to school. Or to even breathe. It was already hard after my mother's death and... Mary, I never expected her to go this soon. Why would god do this to me? Teacher said Mary had to go out for her treatment after the washroom hand incident I witnessed myself. The mirror had been broken in there that day and two of my friends Tina and Mary got their hands accidently injured. It was such a horrific incident to witness. But I didn't expect it to grow into something serious and lead to my best friend's death. After all those things, it was hard

for me to move past them and go on with my life. I still don't feel like it. My life has been miserable since then. I know my stepmom has been really spporting to me in these times just like she always has been. Unlike what I wrote in the story I just wrote. It's really misleading. It was hard for me to write that way but I had to write something creative out of something sensitive. It shattered me when I finally read it. Not only was it just fictional but it was something I would never want to read about. Mary's death. Or me becoming a serial killer. Me turning my step mom into an evil one.

Besides all that, me killing my own best friend Mary? That story was simply damaging. And traumatising. So I wrote another about a one eyed Rottweiler and handed it in instead. I wish I could erase the fact that I wrote such a story from my mind. I wish I could erase the fact that Mary doesn't exist anymore from my mind."

Ryan dropped the diary. He just realised the enormity of what HE did. He killed Betty. He killed his own daughter.

Maybe she actually did all that and wrote the second entry in order to cover her crime. Or maybe not. The first entry could be telling the truth or the second one could be doing so.

Either way, Betty was gone forever.

Just like her mother and Mary were.

III

MR. JAKE'S FUNERAL

3.

Mr. Jake's Funeral

Jake was dead. He was my closest friend, besides being my closest neighbor. He was found stabbed on his kitchen floor.

Nobody knows how he died but everyone was making guesses. Could be a murder, could be a suicide.

The cops had started off with the investigation and had investigated me as well. They suspected his wife, Mrs. Monica, for killing him. And there were many reasons she could have done so.

Mrs. Monica was his second wife. He had remarried after his first wife's death, which was a year ago or so.

I also often used to hear fights from the next door. There seemed to be a lot of family problems in the house. Last year, I heard some glass shattering and Mrs. Monica screaming at 3 A.M. and thought of calling him. I didn't call him though. Jake drove away drunk that night and did not come back for a few days which was strange.

Also, Jake was rich enough, and Monica was greedy enough. And that explained a lot of things.

The most renowned reason out of all was that Mrs. Monica was a baker. She was almost always found in the kitchen, experimenting with the cakes. Jake loved her cakes. And he was found in the kitchen.

Jake had a 13 y/o son from his first wife, Joy. He loved him more than anything in the world. Joy was the reason Jake had remarried. He just wanted him to be happy. Little did he know that Monica brought a lot of abuse with her in the house and that she hated Joy.

Monica had been married before and had her own son, Ron. He was almost the same age as Joy. And Ron and Joy hated each other for some reasons not known.

But at his funeral, they both were unhappy, shocked and traumatised. Ron was crying, like a lot. And Joy was traumatised with his father's demise.

Mrs. Monica was under police investigation.

Jake was found lying on the kitchen floor and was apparently stabbed by someone. Most possibly a sign of murder. But who knows?

They took the knife away for fingerprint scanning. But until then, Monica was behind bars.

When they were done inspecting and the fingerprints on the knife were scanned. They realized it was a murder, and who the murderer was.

It was Joy.

His own son had stabbed him. The cops took Joy with them for further investigation. When they asked why he did what he did, Joy replied-

"Because he said that my step mom Monica baked better cakes than my mom!"

IV

SOMEWHERE ELSE

4.

Somewhere Else

Ellie was stressed. Not only did she fail in her exam, but also failed to impress her parents. She was anxious. What if they slapped her...again? Or worse, what if they abandoned her?

She decided not to tell her parents about this. But that didn't make it any better. Ever since she came to know about her results, all she could do was to over think it.

"Ellie, come make tea for everyone!" She heard someone calling her. Oh that would be her mother, she realised. Her mind was probably somewhere else. She went into the kitchen to do it. Both her mind and her energy were giving in. If only she could order her copy robot to do that for her. Well, she wouldn't have failed then in the first place. She made the tea anyway.

Served it, and ran to her balcony.

She looked up and started crying. There were no birds flying that evening. She could relate to the sky so hard, empty and blue. Then she looked down, she could see peace of mind just 7-8 floors down, if she jumped.

She reached for the railing and put a leg down.

Wait!

Something inside her stopped her. Was she going to commit suicide? No. She couldn't just give up that way. Why would she even think of it? She stopped herself and came up.

She was having that moment of random motivation. Random motivation from the same mind that commanded her to die the other minute.

She was about to go back to her room when,

BAM! The blast threw her out the balcony. 7-8 floors down. Ellie died.

Turns out, she left the stove on while making tea because her mind was somewhere else.

V

LET IT BE A SECRET

5.

Let It Be a Secret

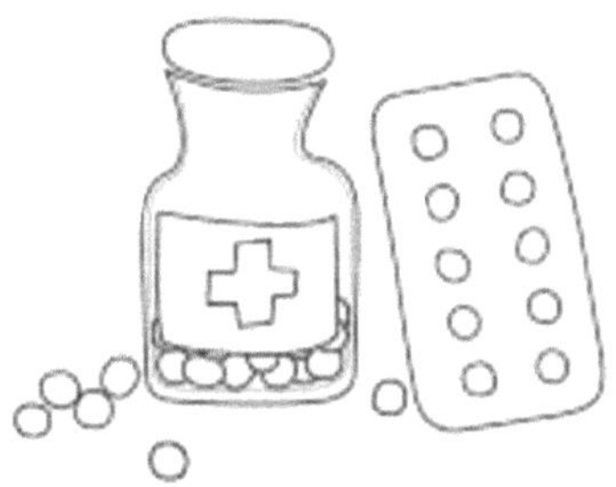

Tim was a sixteen y/o decent boy who hated his father the most.

Not only because his father did drugs, but also because he killed his mother. He gave her some fatal drugs in some conflict and she died.

No, the police did not look into this matter for some reason. And the store owner was his father's friend who sold him such drugs. Tim had been living with that secret since he was small.

He knew what happened. He saw what happened. He just couldn't do anything about it.

He hated the fact that drugs existed, and that his mother didn't.

But his mother used to tell him to be nice to everyone. And he really was, extremely kind and generous to everyone. But not everyone treated him that way. He felt like everyone hated him.

He had a friend Lily who probably hated him the most in the world, if we exclude his father from the expression. Lily's mother was about to marry Tim's father. And that was possibly the reason she hated him. Maybe because she was intuitive about Tim's father. Well, Tim was always good to her anyway because his mother taught him so.

Lily hated the fact that her mother and his father were about to get married. Tim did too. But he knew how his father was, he knew he could do nothing about his marraige.

Lily had talked to her mother about that several times though. But that didn't seem to work. Tim's father knew that Lily hated him. So he hated her as well.

A few weeks to their wedding!

No, Lily couldn't accept the fact that they were getting married. That was the last thing she wanted to happen and She did not want Tim as her step brother, she could not hate him more.

Lily knew she could do nothing about it at that point. Tim was unsettled about the marriage as well, but he had his reasons to not speak up.

But not anymore. Not when Lily abused his mother.

Yes, he was used to his father abusing his mother back when she was alive, when he hadn't killed her. But he could no longer see Lily say such thing about his late mother.

His mother had always been nice to everybody. His mother never deserved those things.

Never deserved the husband she got. Or whatever that Lily girl had to say about her. His mother never deserved the death she got.

LILY DESERVED THAT.

He ran to the store his father used to go to. Trying to think of some way, the store owner could sell him the fatal drugs. To kill Lily. He hated her. She deserved that. His mother didn't.

He was in the store. And he stopped. He hid somewhere. Not because he didn't know what to ask from that owner. Not because he didn't know what to do. But because he knew exactly what to do at that point.

He ran to the nearest police station and gave them the voice note he had recorded of his father talking to the store owner. Talking about drugging Lily to kill her. Because she hated him and he hated her.

Police arrested his father right away and informed Lily's mother about it all. Tim saved Lily. And Lily and her mother couldn't be more grateful.

Yes, He hated Lily. But he couldn't hate her more than he hated his father.

Lily asked Tim why he went to that store in the first place.

"Let it be a secret, Lily." Tim replied.

VI

HIS TRUE IDENTITY

6.

His True Identity

Josh was on the stage, speaking in front of a thousand college students who listened to him with utter concentration. There was a high chance that if he told the crowd that Michael Jackson was his family and he just visited his grave with Kentucky Fried Chickens instead of a rose they would have believed him. Not that funny joke, he knew.

He had no connection with him, though. And that wasn't why he was there. He was called there to address the college students on his beliefs and his concerns. He was a well known public speaker and everybody in the crowd seemed to like him. And they seemed to be intrigued by whatever he spoke.

"You came with nothing and you'll leave with nothing. There is not even a single thing in this world that you take with your grave, with the exception of your own existence. And in the end, when you're gone, nobody will realise what all things have gone with you.

Nobody will know who the real you was, because we tend to never actually show our true selves. We talk about grave secrets and all, but you know that the biggest grave secret you're taking with yourself is you. When you die, you take your true identity with you."

Josh ended his speech with this and asked for questions from the audience. Seemed like everyone was satisfied with his speech. Or bored. They didn't look like they were bored though. Thank god, he thought.

Right when Josh felt nobody had any questions and considered the job there done, a student raised his hand.

"You're talking about every human right? Don't you count yourself in? Do you not hide your real identity or do you consider yourself an exception?" The student asked.

"Well, I got nothing to hide buddy. I'm a simple man, I speak what I feel is right. I have a wife and almost 3 kids. As in, my wife is going to deliver our third kid today. That's why I'm so excited to end this speech and run to the hospital where my family is right now. I have nothing to hide. I'm pretty much an exception." Josh replied.

"Okay I'll consider you an exception. Although, we really don't know the truth because, as you said, you would have taken your real self with you."

"Well, I guess when I die and if there is such a thing as an afterlife, you will know my true self and that I haven't lied about a single thing on this stage." Josh replied with a smile on his face and went away.

When he was driving his car to the adoption centre. Not a hospital but an adoption centre, He checked his wife's texts to realise she was already there and there was only a couple of minutes before they welcomed a new family member.

He was overjoyed with that one text and he turned his car toward the destination without realising that there was a truck behind and without realising that he was on a huge bridge.

His car bumped into the truck and found itself spinning around thrice and diving deep into the water.

Josh died that day. His car sank in the water. The machines took Josh and his car out. His body headless, his soul lifeless.

The doctors did his post mortem as his family demanded. Turns out, he did have his own secrets.

Because he was a Trans man.

VII

THE LAST DAY

7.

The Last Day

Sally, a 20 years old girl, was used to getting abused by her little brother. Well, know that there's a big difference between annoying and abusing. And this story is not about a sibling fight!

Her brother Miles was a 17 something pampered kid. Everybody in the house loved him. Everybody in the world loved him. In fact, Sally loved him too.

Even after whatever she used to go through because of him, she always had some space in her heart for her brother. And it had nothing to do with him but her.

One day, Sally was doing whatever she had to, and Miles was doing whatever he could to irritate someone, Sally.

So he snatched her phone away, deleted all the contacts, photos and whatever he could get to.

As soon as Sally saw him doing this, she snatched her phone back from him and opened the sim tray to check if he had done anything to it. Yep. She opened the tray and found water inside. Miles had put water in the speakers.

She took a heavy breath, wondering what more she could take in from her not so little brother.

No, it was not funny. She screamed at him. Crying, already.

Nobody had ever talked to Miles like that. Not even their parents. No one. Miles was extremely angry at her.

He slapped her. Yes. He did. Now the descriptions feels like a sibling quarrel, but believe the writer, the story isn't.

Sally felt an immediate urge to hit him with the cricket bat she could see near her, not just for what he did with her phone but what things he had always done to her. She did not, though. She threw a book at him instead. Not with the intention to hurt him, but to feed her own anger.

She had never been angry enough to hit someone with things. But how long could she take it in. Although, Miles did take the cricket bat from near Sally and hit her back with it.

She was bleeding and crying. Miles was crying too. She hit him with a book. She shouted at him. How could she?

That was when their father entered the room. He noticed Milles was crying. His son was crying. He asked what it was about. And Miles explained. Everything. From what he did to her phone to why he was crying. His father turned mad.

"He wouldn't have slapped you for no reason, Sally. Who's older? I see who the problem here is." He said.

No he did not. The problem wasn't Sally. The problem wasn't Miles either. Maybe, it was him. Because Sally never knew where she went wrong. He had done even worse and unbearable things to her, but it was not what he did at that point, it was what his father had said.

She stormed off, ignoring his father's "come back here or you are dead!" because she knew there was no point of explaining anything to him.

She was done.

She was running to her room when she heard her father scream before her.

"That's it. I'm no longer tolerating this girl's demeanour. She has to learn how to respect her father." He screamed.

He took out his belt and ran to her room. Screaming- "This is the last day you ever disrespect your father, Sally."

Too late,

Sally had already cut her wrist from the rounder, that Miles had kept on her bed to poke her.

VIII

RIGHT WHERE THEY CHAT AND EAT

8.

Right Where They Chat and Eat

I'm trembling.

I can see the plate in front of me. I can see the food. I can see my death in front of me. I can't. I can't eat it. I know for sure that I would throw up.

It's not like I'm trying to lose weight. I'm trying to gain instead. This, according to others is no big deal, but I don't know what's wrong with me. I wish it actually was that easy for me. I wish I weren't here, having a panic attack and pretending like I just don't feel like eating. Like I just don't eat much. It's better than accepting the fact that I eat and eat and eat until I remember I'm messed up from the inside.

That girl haunts me every time I look into the mirror. I cannott stand her anymore.

Okay, let's not forget there are other people on this table. Let's pretend to eat at least. I'm totally full. I already ate so much pasta last night. I'm sick of pasta now. And here it is, in front of my eyes on the table.

I thought I could gain weight in a day and look better, less skinny at the party I'm at right now. It didn't seem to work. So I had to wear 5 layers of clothing. Hoping it doesn't look obvious. Wishing it was some different season instead of summer.

What more excuses do I have down my sleeves now? I guess it's too late for "I actually ate today!" , because the food is right here in front of me. Laughing at me, at how helpless I feel, how terribly conscious I am about this food. More conscious about how others are thinking of me, to be honest.

My hands are shaking. I pick up the fork. Play with the pasta. Check my phone while others are busy chatting and..Well, eating.

Someone looked at me and said something. I can't figure out what. Probably, "Look at you, you need to eat!" To which my regular reply is, "Don't we all?"

They think I don't eat. I actually don't, for days after I eat like crazy with just one motive, until my body says no and I'm not able to eat straight for a few days, surviving only on liquids. My appetite is very much screwed. So am I.

I'm just sitting here, randomly remembering that one time I went to my relative's and came back thinking I needed to put on some weight or die. Every time someone brings up this topic, that's all I feel like doing. And I'll never blame them for body shaming because look at me, that's all I do looking in the mirror to myself. They remind me that I'm skinny as if I'm not already aware. As if the mirror hasn't already told me that. As if I don't cry looking into the mirror because WHO THE HELL IS THIS SKINNY?

My mind brings me back to the table and I realise I'm the only one here. Everyone else is done with their food, long before I even noticed, probably thinking I'm a slow eater when in actuality I'm just messed up.

I'm the only one here left with my food. God didn't give me a normal appetite. God gave me THIS *body. The one I hate but act like I really don't care what they all say about.*

I get up from my table leaving the plate on its own. Feeling bad about leaving food, the thing so many people die because they don't get.

But feeling worse about myself. Then feeling selfish and narcissistic the next minute.

Feeling like I'm being boiled alive, because of how suffocated I am in the 5 layer clothing I have worn.

Taking support of what I think feels like a wall. Lying down to what I think feels like a death bed, until my eyes roll back and faint to black.

PS: LOL THIS ONE HAS NO DIALOGUES AND KINDA NO GOOD PLOT AS WELL BUT IT'S ONE OF MY FAVS. *or not.*

IX

THE SAND DIGGER

9.

The Sand Digger

Jim and Michael were best buds!

Jim used to run toward Michael as soon as Michael used to get a break from his construction work, wagging his tail and licking his face.

Michael was a construction site worker and Jim was a stray dog. Both were homeless. They both had known each other for a year when Michael found an abandoned pup on the construction site and named him Jim.

They used to play together and live together at the construction site. Michael didn't have any family either so that made them the best duo ever. Jim used to run toward Michael as soon as he used to get a break from his work, taking a break from his own work of digging the sand cliff on the site.

Every other worker knew about that bond and they didn't seem to mind much. But the Contractor Andy did, since Michael played with Jim more than he worked. It never bothered Michael. All that mattered to him was Jim.

One day, the duo was minding their own fun when Andy barged in and yelled at Michael for not doing his work on working hours. He did have a valid reason to yell though, it was only fair. But the fact that Andy also threatened Michael to kill Jim or throw him away was not.

It was more than just about animal rights for Michael. Michael started working because he was homeless and poor but well, Jim became everything for Michael. he didn't know that he would get a reason to earn. Jim was his only family.

So Michael stopped ditching his work because losing his only job wasn't really sensible. Andy still seemed to mind the dog though. Yelling at Michael and throwing rocks at Jim became his personal entertainment.

And then all the workers started hating the dog as well. Because you know, got to follow the boss.

One night, Michael slept, wondering why everyone would want to snatch the only best thing in his life from him. It was very dark that night, all the workers and Jim were sleeping when Jim suddenly woke up. He felt a stone prick him.

He looked up to see Andy looking down at him. With a knife in his hand.

He turned around in order to run away but Andy grabbed him and held him high. As insensitively as he could.

Jim was up in the air trying to get himself free when he felt a jerk from behind and fell down. He ran as fast as he could and didn't come back until morning. He came back next morning, only for Michael. Dogs. Loyalty.

That morning, when Jim was passionately digging his sand cliff, he found Andy's dead body inside.

P.S: I WROTE THIS ONE BACK WHEN I HAD JUST STARTED WATCHING THE OFFICE, APPARENTLY.

X

UNDER MY STEP

10.

Under My Step

I was going back home late at night. I used to do night shifts in my office every night. It was a chilly November night with a sudden and unexpected temperature fall. I had not brought a jacket with me and knew there was no way I could survive the night without one.

So to survive the night I decided to go out and get a jacket from any random clothing store that could be open at that hour. I walked out of my office and after a few minutes of walking, found a clothing store.

I walked in there and saw a saleswoman working. She seemed almost my age doing a night shift just like me. She was the only one there and I just felt like having a small talk with her, so we did.

But the small talk turned out to be a cool stranger talk and I felt like I could share anything with Aurora, the saleswoman. I genuinely felt so nice talking to her and Aurora seemed less like a stranger and more like a long lost friend.

As we chatted, I came to know that she lived alone as well, just like I did, did night shifts in the store and we had so much more in common.

After about half an hour of talking about our worlds, I decided to look at what I was there for. I asked for a jacket or something warm to her and she immediately handed me a white cardigan with black buttons on it.

I looked at it. It looked pretty. I looked at her to ask what she thought of it.

That was the moment I realised it was similar to the one she was wearing. She was wearing the same cardigan and to be honest I found the twinning cool.

Aurora said she found it extremely comfortable and with that cardigan on, she never once felt sad and alone. That made sense since I lived alone too. I could emphatically relate to her so I bought it.

We talked more and more and she told me about the pet rat she had for a few years that died the very morning because she accidently stepped on it. And I told her about the pet parrot I used to have as a kid. We talked a bit more about our personal lives and the way we felt about living alone and doing night shifts before I went back to my office wearing it and feeling the most comfortable I had ever been.

I went back home wearing it. And went to sleep, still wearing it. That was the most comfortable sleep ever.

The next day, I woke up. With my head throbbing and my eyes burning as if I had not just woken up from a sleep. I sat on my bed, only to see that the cardigan I had been wearing all night was on the floor,

Smeared in blood.

I stood up, horror-struck.

I felt something. Something under my step. It was a dead rat.

I panicked. Not knowing what to do, what had to be done. I went to the washroom. Looked in the mirror.

There it was, I had it on. I had the cardigan on me.

But the person wearing it wasn't me. It was Aurora.

With blood all over her face. My face.

BASED ON A TRUE STORY

(MANDATORY STATEMENT TO ADD)

XI

AT THE STRIKE OF 11

11.

At the Strike of 11

I was sitting on my couch after dinner, scrolling through my phone. The clock struck eleven. And I almost went to bed when I heard some noise from outside. The walls were pretty thin.

I heard a man's voice and a woman's heels. His voice wasn't clear enough to understand him but his whistling were. It was quite enough to hear those whistling and I was smart enough to know what was going on out there, especially at that hour. But I could do nothing about it. Well, except for over thinking it.

I lived alone, I could certainly not do anything alone so there was no point in getting into such a fuss. But I couldn't over think more about it because it happened the next night as well. And the next of it too.

A week passed of me constantly hearing some street harassment happen and doing absolutely nothing about it. Nope. Not anymore.

I made up my mind that I would be calling the police for help the very minute I heard those voices again. That night I didn't scroll through my phone thinking I could do nothing about it. Because I could.

I did hear those whistling and heels again later that night, exactly at the strike of eleven. I stepped out to warn the guy first. Calling the police was my backup option.

But what I saw instead was a lady whistling at the stray dogs to feed them at night.

Every night, at the strike of eleven.

XII

TIME, MYSTICAL TIME

12.

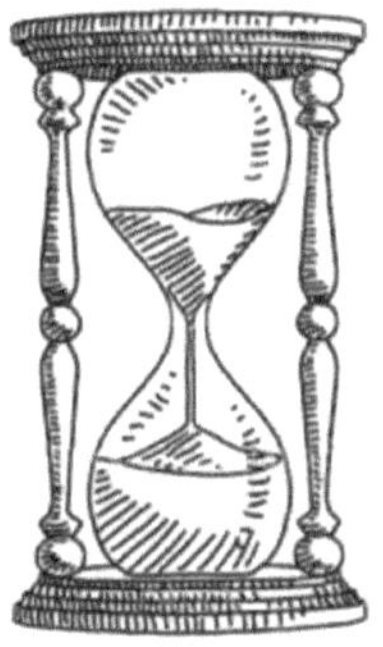

Time, Mystical Time

That clock was cursed. It had some strong powers. I could feel them. That was one 50 years old antique clock that my grandpa used to have back then. But I was not just saying. I could prove that it was cursed, I had reasons.

My grandpa died because he couldn't tolerate the noise that the clock made. He already had a brain stroke problem. And my father, he committed suicide because that clock didn't wake him up for a flight. He didn't just miss his flight, but also missed the last chance to see his mother at her funeral. He couldn't see her for one last time. And that was the kind of guilt you never want to have. That clock had taken my father and my grandpa from me. It did have some powers, I believed. I went to sleep with that thought on my mind.

The next morning, I woke up. And as soon as I did, my mom asked me to buy some groceries. I refused to go, So she had to go there herself. Then I took the clock and threw it into the bin. End of drama ... I guess?

I was doing my homework when I got the news that my mom had died due to a car accident on her way. No....just...no! I ran to the hospital.

Saw her, touched her for one last time, tried to wake her up, begged her to come back, but she was long gone.

Why would god do this to me? He snatched grandpa, grandma, father and then mother from me. He might hate me a lot. Do I have nobody left in my life now?

Only if I hadn't refused to go. Only if I could turn back time.

I cried. I kept crying until I heard the alarm clock. I vaguely remembered throwing it away. I woke up and saw my mother sitting beside me.

She was crying, trying to wake me up, begging me to come back. But I was long gone.

PS: YES, IT'S FROM A GHOST'S POV, FOCUS ON THE STORY PLEASE!

XIII

13 YEARS GONE

13.

13 Years Gone..

Jase was dancing.

He got into his dream college he always wanted to get into. He had dreamt of that day his whole life and that was the moment he could finally look forward to a great future, beyond all his pasts and childhood traumas. He knew achieving his dream could heal him. But that not only healed him, that made him the happiest he had ever been.

His family threw a party to celebrate his accomplishments. They were ecstatic and proud of Jase. He felt proud of himself as well. He worked hard enough and finally made it all the way up. His parents invited everyone they knew. His mother wanted every single person they knew to celebrate her son's accomplishment. And so many of them did come.

They were all congratulating him and his parents. Jase could not have been any prouder of himself. Because it was a party meant just for him.

Then he saw an old lady. She smiled and came toward him and his mother.

"Hey. You might not remember me, Jase." She said. He did.

"Hello, Miss Miller. I'm so glad that you came." Jase's mother greeted her.

"How could I not? I had to see this kid succeed. After all, he had been my student. And apart from all, I had to congratulate you for being such a great and supportive mother. You made all this happen." Miss Miller said.

Jase kept staring between the two.

"No, it was you who made this happen. You were the teacher who taught him the very basics. He stammered so much as a kid, you made him speak. He used to get failed, you made him excel. I'm so glad I made him join tuitions when he was 8"; Jase's mother replied. Jase was quiet.

"No, he was just 8. I'm sure he doesn't even remember me teaching him or anything about it, for that matter." Miss Miller smiled at him.

That was the moment Jase could not hold it in anymore. He ran away. Trying not to show his emotions. Trying not to show that he was crying, just like his 8 year old self used to.

Because he did. He remembered it. He remembered it all.

He remembered when he used to stammer and Miss Miller used to hit him with a stick on his knuckles because he did not stop with his "stammering thing".

Jase ran to the washroom. He remembered it.

He remembered when he complained about that to his mother but she never cared because at least he was improving his speech from his fear of getting beaten up.

Jase locked himself in the washroom. He remembered it.

When he could not walk back to his house because Miss Miller made him kneel down for 2 hours straight because he wouldn't stop with his stammering and failed in tests. Jase was crying.

He was crying because he remembered that one time when Miss Miller pulled down his pants in front of all those laughing kids and his mother, who won't do anything about it because she wanted him to never fail a test.

He remembered it. He remembered it all.

PS: I had to fight the overpowering urge to name her Miss Killer instead of Miss Miller.

XIV

THE HALLOWEEN NIGHT

14.

The Halloween Night

It was Halloween night and I was working late. The clock struck 1 when I left my workplace and started walking back to my house. I was walking on a bridge that connected my neighborhood to my office.

It was very dark and a bit scary because I felt someone behind me. I heard heels but whenever I turned back there was no sign of anyone behind. I bit my lips hard and kept going.

I figured it could be someone trying to scare me since it was Halloween. At Least I hoped so. I resumed walking and heard those heels again. But looked back to find no one. Just streetlights fluttering and my heart racing. I kept on with my walk and my lip biting.

Afraid I might be in trouble, I thought of taking a cab but there wasn't any at that hour and my app wasn't working. All the bad things seemed to happen at the same time. So I continued walking and guess what? I heard those heels again. I bit my lips harder until I could taste my blood.

I was afraid to turn around at that point. But I did. And that time, I spotted someone. There was a girl my age in an angel's costume and blue heels, the one that made the noise that scared me. Probably returning from a Halloween party. Never was I that relieved in my life to see a girl. But it was still dark and scary.

I knew she was walking just behind me because I felt her walking awfully close to me. Then I heard a noise again. I turned around. Not heels though. Just a truck honking.

I saw the truck moving toward me but it was far enough. The truck was less of an issue since I couldn't find the Angel dressed girl.

She was walking just inches apart from me a minute ago, but then, she was just gone. There was no sign of her. I couldn't believe my own eyes. I lost my senses. There was no place she could hide. We were on a bridge. There was no road she could have possibly taken, no car she might have gotten in.

I didn't notice the Angel dressed girl getting away until she was gone. Neither did I notice the truck coming that close until it hit me.

I flew out of the bridge, but was holding on that railing, death gripped. until my hands were burning and I was slipping down. It was so hard to keep myself from falling but I knew that if I fell, I wouldn't get up dusting myself off. I then saw the angel-dressed girl run toward me.

She gave me a hand to pull me. I took it. I was lifting up, before falling down. When I was about to reach up, she withdrew her hand. And as I was falling to my death, I looked up and saw that the angel dressed girl wasn't in an angel's costume anymore

....but a devil's one.

XV

SHE KEPT IT

15.

She Kept It

Ava, an 18 y/o girl, was in the kitchen, chopping vegetables for dinner. When she paused, just paused chopping them. She was chopping spinach. Her sister used to hate it, out of all the other things she used to hate. She realised she was holding a knife. But surely not the one her sister had used a year ago to kill herself. It was still sharp, useful, could cut veggies, or her entire family which seemed to be the reason why her sister had to kill herself.

She wished she could stab them all, especially her grandfather. If Ava had gotten a chance to kill her family, she would have taken it. And it was alright because she knew if her family were given a chance to kill her, she knew they would have killed her.

She had always been the minor and the least liked child in the family and as dark as it sounds, the only one surviving. Because, they had already killed the most liked one.

But Ava was very much alive, chopping and thinking about her long gone sister and the way her family had made it seem like an accident, her sister's suicide.

No, there were no ghosts there, but her house was still cursed.

She continued with her cooking, not wanting to ruin anything and disappoint the grandfather but also wanting to ruin the whole meal. Maybe some poison could do.

But that was all in her head. She could never do anything above thinking about killing them.

The next day was her marriage. She was just 18, hadn't even graduated yet. But her grandpa had forced her into marrying against her will, just what they did to her sister. Sure, she had her rights as a human. But obviously if she could do something against it, she would have done it. She knew the consequences of speaking up better than anyone else.

And there you are on your bed, not able to get your "beauty sleep" the night before your wedding. Wondering what had to be done in order to save yourself.

The day finally comes. You look at yourself in the mirror, finding yourself in your wedding dress. The ugliest you could ever look or feel.

You look out the window and watch your family greet the guests. You come back to the dresser. Still not aware what had to be done. You pull the first drawer. Pick up the earrings and get it on. Then pull the last drawer and take the knife out.

But this time, the one your sister did use to kill herself from.

XVI

WHAT WAS THAT?

16. *What Was That?*

I was running to catch a butterfly in the garden. The butterfly was the most beautiful thing I had ever seen and the 10 year old me definitely wanted to catch it.

It was late in the evening and I was alone. I had actually come all by myself there because none of my cousins were interested in playing with me. I was at my granny's house and I knew my way to the garden and back.

I had no trouble playing alone. That was just something I always did at home, but better there in the garden. The garden was as big as I could imagine. I used to think it covered half of the city, even though it didn't. That was just what a 10 year old me had wondered. But it had still covered a huge part of the neighborhood. The guard over there never minded his business. As in, he was always roaming around not caring about his duty. But it didn't matter to me because he had once called me a sweet girl. I didn't mind if he went around not caring about his job. I liked him.

And there I was, a tiny 10 year old me, running behind a butterfly, trying to enclose it in my hands. I was so into it that I never realised when I bumped into a palm tree and fell head first to some bricks.

Yes, I fainted. It was worse than it sounds. Because when I opened my eyes, my head throbbed in pain, my eyes were already watery and I knew I was bleeding. I looked around. Only to see....nobody.

The park got closed. The guard never checked in on me. He never cared about the sweet girl, or the job. He never deserved my "best guard in the World" card or the flower rings I made him.

I was crying, because it hurt to walk but I needed to get out of there. Then I cried more because I knew my granny and cousins didn't know I was there. It was dark.

I was walking around in the garden I had imagined covered half of the city. There was no way I could jump off the 25 feet railing, the one I called the Great Wall of China as a joke. It didn't seem funny when the 10 y/o me was trying to escape the same wall.

I saw the door to the compost area. I knew it had been locked ever since I could remember. It was always empty because the gardeners never opened it. Also, it had a "Do not enter" sign that the 10 year old me could of course read, but not in the dark.

Given that the fence surrounding the cubical sized compartment for the compost or whatever, was not as giant as the Great Wall of China, I climbed it and jumped off it.

I didn't know what I was doing but it was certainly not a way to my home. I saw a square shaped huge manhole in it, which was useless since what was it there for?

And obviously I did NOT jump off it, I slipped.

And the moment I hit the ground, I thought I had died already. I had a feeling I was going to be trapped in there forever. Forever, until my death. I knew I was going to die there and nobody was ever going to find my corpse.

I thought I knew what darkness was. But being trapped in a garden at night with the streetlights on was definitely not it.

I thought I knew that gardens were nothing more than playing hide and seek and hiding under the bushes until found or catching a butterfly, until I couldn't anymore.

But then I realised there were thousands of fireflies lighting the whole damn place. I saw something, a big giant gold lion statue. And I heard something, water.

I went on to see a huge waterfall there. It led to what seemed like a deadly lake. Not because it had bloody water or something, but the crocodiles.

I realised crocodiles weren't the only thing to be scared of, the giant lion itself had hundreds of bats stuck upside down to it. And there were spider webs in the air. The whole place wasn't just spooky. It was death dealing. It felt like I was seeing my own death.

I felt something cold touch me, grab me, and pull me into the water. I looked down. Not the crocodiles, the pods grabbing my legs and taking me with them. And the moment when I got pulled into the water knowing there were crocodiles in there was when I considered myself dead.

Death by slipping into the water.

Death by slipping off the manhole.

Death by catching a butterfly.

And in that moment, I woke up. Not in the water or a dark underground village. Not even in the garden. I saw myself in a hospital bed.

"Oh thank god, we almost lost you!" was what the doctor said.

What was that? The whole thing?

After a few minutes of gaining my consciousness, the doctor came to check in on me again.

"You fainted in the garden and got some minor head injuries but I think you will be fine after some time. This man brought you here." The doc pointed to the guard who was sitting near me.

I think he deserved the card and the flower ring!

XVII

UP IN THE AIR

17.

Up In The Air

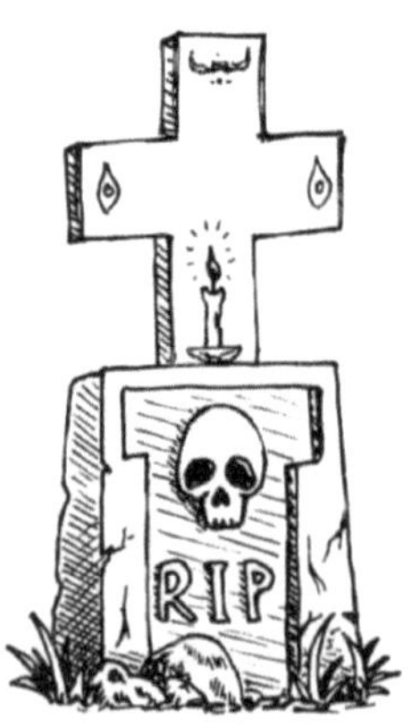

My sister was there down in the basement, looking at the antiques that our granny had left behind. We lived in our granny's house in the city of New York. Just me and my sister.

I had never really seen my granny though. I was like 5 years old when she died so I have no memory of her. All I knew of her was the house we lived in and that one photograph of her with my mother.

They were always smiling in that picture. No, I did not remember any of her memories. But why did I remember my granny hitting my mother and making her cry?

Though, whenever I looked back at the photograph, they looked happy. Always smiling.

When I was younger, I used to ask my mother if that was true, if granny actually did such things to her. But she used to refuse that each time. There wasn't really a valid reason for me to hate granny. And no, I did not hate her. But I didn't like her either. No apparent reason.

On the contrary, my sister loved granny. She did remember clear memories of playing with her when she was a kid. She loved her.

I went to the basement. My sister looked at me. "Hey. How are you? Hope you remember what day today is."

"Not really. Why?" I replied. Of course, I did.

"Oh my god, It is Granny's death anniversary today. We both will be going to the churchyard to fresh her grave with flowers and farewell greetings." My sister said, holding one of granny's pictures in her hand.

She was crying already. Oh, how much she might love her. "Um, I know how much it means to you. But I kinda don't want to go there." I replied.

"What do you mean? You have to go there with me. Not like she would want a granddaughter like you there who refused to visit her grave." She said, still looking at the photographs, her skin turning red with anger.

"It isn't about her. Graveyards are not really my thing." I replied, knowing that made no sense.

"Not your thing? That is your granny you're talking about. I knew you never liked her." She shouted, finally looking at me with red eyes.

"Ok, let me put it straight. I'm not going there. And I don't care if her soul haunts me now. Mom never really visited her and I won't either." I shouted back. "Yah and mom died, didn't she?" I heard my sister saying.

I looked at her red face, she was staring at me with a whole new pair of dark red eyes. I turned around and started walking away........until I couldn't anymore.

My sister grabbed my neck from behind, choking me. I could not breathe at all. Then she held me up in the air, my feet inches from the ground.

"Please, stop!" I managed to say, choking to death.

Then she rotated me so that I could face my sister, who was crying looking at grandma's photos.

Not knowing that I was dying,

Up in the air.

XVIII

THE WATER

18.

The Water

Here I am. On the verge of a panic attack. Also, of a swimming pool.

It's my swimming class today in school. I have been avoiding or bunking this class since the last 8 years of my school. But today, I had no choice but to get in this swimming pool and watch myself die. I'm not hydrophobic. I'm just terrified of water.

It suffocates me, the water.

Wish these people knew my story. Nope. They never should. I was 8 when my mom adopted me and ever since then my life has been no less than a happy fairytale. I'm so happy I have the family I have now. Not that my old one was appalling. But it has been 8 years. And my new one is keeping me happy enough to forget whatever my old one was.

I was 8 years old when I was on a road trip with my family. My father was driving. My mother on the passenger side, and me on the back. It was dark. I had my head in the cloud. Watching the trees, the mountains, and the stalking moon before I passed out to the jerk of that one accident. Only if my father hadn't fallen asleep while driving. But he did

As I was losing consciousness, I was losing my family. But when I gained consciousness, the family was still lost. Could never gain it back.

I opened my eyes. My mother had her head smeared in blood. And my father had his on the steering wheel. I screamed. But it didn't seem to wake the deceased. Only I had my seatbelt on. But what was the point of it? It sure saved me, but at what cost.

I was looking at the two bodies ahead of me. Scanning them in search of any soul left. My father had surely left long before I gained my consciousness back. But my mother's fingers motioned.

She was alive. I wasn't the only one surviving the accident. My mother was alive.

I took off my seatbelt and reached for her. Without realising that my one swift movement could lead to my mother's death. Without realising that the car wasn't in any place steady. Car was hanging off a cliff, before I made that movement. After, it was diving deep. Deep into the water.

It suffocated me, the water.

It snatched my breath and got me fighting for it. The water made me slowly lose consciousness again. Thinking I could never get it back. But I did. Because I never lost it again.

I felt my mother touching me. She was there behind me. She held my hands as we searched our way up the water. We were at the very bottom, or at least it felt like it.

Without any words, she gestured to me to hold my breath. So I did. Hoping she could speak to tell me it was really her, alive and speaking to me. Not knowing that speaking anything could kill her or me at that point. Dumb 8 y/o. Still alive when her mother was dying.

She held my hands until she couldn't anymore. I never let her go but I felt her go away. I felt another hand behind me. Not my father's. Certainly not my mother's.

I looked at her as the hands dragged me out of the water. I couldn't hear them. Couldn't hear anything apart from water. Water has its voice. And it stifles yours.

Our hands were released. And she was gone.

The next thing I knew I was in the hospital. Getting pricked by something. And I started losing consciousness again. I didn't want to. I tried my best to beat that drug. Anyone who has enough in them to try to fight an anesthesia knows you don't fade to black. You just look at the ceiling above your hospital bed until it all slowly turns to white. I faded to white.

I'm standing near the swimming pool. Head back in the cloud. Until the swimming teacher pushes me in. I'm in the water again.

It suffocates me, the water. It snatches my breath and gets me fighting for it yet again.

I feel my mother touching me. She is there behind me. She holds my hands as we search our way up the water. We are at the very bottom, or at least it feels like it.Without any word, she gestures to me to hold my breath. So I do it.

Hoping she can speak to tell me it's really her, alive and speaking to me. Not knowing that speaking anything can kill her or me at this point. Dumb 16 y/o me. Still alive when her mother isn't.

I feel another hand on me, dragging me out.

I hold her gaze until our hands are released. And she is gone.

But with a smile on her face this time.

XIX

REBEKAH

19.

I'm in my daughter Rebekah's room. Wait... Let's start it all over again.

I'm in my daughter, Dr. Rebekah Hope's room thinking about how my dear little Daisy escalated from fainting by just a view of blood to becoming a surgeon. I mean I'm so proud of her.

Everything about her makes me feel proud of her. She has been through so much in her childhood and just looking at how she never let those things sidetrack her makes me want to climb whatever the tallest tower is and scream her name till everybody out there knows how proud I am.

I mean, I love my daughter so much. I know my daughter is a surgeon now but she went through hell of a nightmare in her teenage years. She had sleep walking issues since forever but when she was 12, her sleepwalking became a big deal and I remember feeling like the worst mom ever because I saw her go through such things and couldn't do anything. We were a joint family at that time, and I felt like nobody could do anything to save my little girl.

One night, she sleepwalked and found her way to the mirror. She had unconsciously punched the mirror and those tiny pieces cut her hand, the one she now uses to perform surgeries.

We all ran to her room that day afraid she might have hurt herself, which she did. Her uncle was the first one to reach her and after that night I felt like fitting a CCTV camera in her room but that seemed an absurd option to explore. So we never did that.

Apart from that, she had injured herself a lot by falling down the staircase, thrice. And going out of the house to the nearest bookstore only to be brought back by the store owner himself. She liked writing poetries. She went through a whole phase of poetry writing that time.

I'm pretty sure if the surgeon thing would have not worked out, she would be the biggest poet of them all. But well, now she's the best surgeon of them all. Although she stopped writing poetries when she entered high school.

Ah, I miss my girl so much. She was 12 when we had to send her to therapy after she had that one life threatening incident, back in the destructive sleepwalking phase.

She had sleep walked across the hall to the kitchen and when she opened her eyes, she found herself laying right there. Near her uncle's dead body.

That was the moment she got the biggest trauma of her life. She screamed and ran to our rooms and I remember running to her thinking she hurt herself but finding her uncle dead instead.

We realised he had slipped down the oily floor in the kitchen and slammed his head on one of the cabinets. It was a tough time for all of us. But especially for Rebekah.

I think it's all okay now that my daughter is a successful rich doctor and has no sleepwalking issues. My daughter is a fighter and I'll always be proud of her.

I was trying to find the poetries she had written in her room but god, that room needed some cleaning. I may or may not have become a lazy mother after I lost my daughter to the Medical College.

Ah found them, the poetries! I was going to read through them all no matter how long it was going to take me to decode her messy handwriting. No wonder she's a doctor. Surgeon, whatever.

I kept flipping through the pages, reading all the beautiful pieces of poetry my daughter had ever written until I reached the last page.

THE MIRROR SAW IT ALL

I'm awake all night. Scared of my terrible
sleepwalking issue.

Staring into my reflection until I see one more
show up. I look at my uncle standing just
behind me.

Not knowing what his intentions were until he
showed them.

He muffled my scream. Had to punch a hole in the mirror.

In hopes I could save myself from the sinking.

Too late, I'm drowning now.

I read this one poem again and again. Then I flipped the page to read the last one dated on the day his uncle had died. I knew I didn't want to read it already. The title was already tear stained. Not mine.

There I am, gaining consciousness. Then screaming my lungs out the next minute.

Ignoring that he didn't fall, but was pushed. Acting like I didn't faint with the view of blood, but sleepwalked.

Nice to have a disease to blame on.

I forced my watery eyes to read the tear stained title.

JUST WANTED TO GET SOME WATER

More tears stained the paper.

This time mine.

PS: IK THE POEMS ARENT RHYMING BUT IM NOT GOOD AT IT SO I'LL LEAVE IT ON "POETIC FREEDOM" hehe

XX

ABOVE ME

20.

Above Me

Just above my bed was a fan. Whenever I opened my eyes after a nap, the first thing coming in to my view was that fan. Not that it was a creepy fan because it was such a fancy one that my mom's grandfather had sent. It looked like a pretty old one. It had some kind of wind chime on it, so that it could give optimistic vibes every time I turned it on. My mother told me though that she would remove it till summer.

It looked pretty fancy. If you looked closer you could see a portrait of a Japanese lady with a white fox. The only thing that creeped me out was that the Japanese lady had no legs. It was made to portray the breakout of some limb disorder. But it was still cool to have an antique fan in my room, just above my head all the time.

It was extremely cold so I wore my sweater, my gloves, my pair of socks and every winter necessities. I didn't usually wear sweaters and socks when I slept but those nights were so cold, I mean I didn't want to be frozen dead while I was asleep. So I did it.

The next day I woke up and jumped out of bed. Oh my god, the floor was freezing cold. Wait, where were my socks? I looked at the bed. There they were. I thought I wore them.

Some really weird things happened to me later that day. I caught a cold. That was it. Not much. I wore socks that night too. And woke up, with none.

I searched for them. They were not on the bed. Where were they?The wind chime above me rang. I looked up.

My socks were hanging there on the fan. I stood on my bed to take them off. Wait.....were my ankles bleeding? But it didn't hurt at all. It was probably a mosquito. It had to be.

I reached for the socks and noticed something strange. The Japanese lady, her hands were covered in blood. That was too horrifying. It might have been there ever since and I might not have noticed. No other explaination.

The day started strangely and ended the same. I tripped in the washroom. It was already hard for me to work in winters and my clumsiness was making it harder.

The wind chime rang. That was becoming irritating. So I removed it real quick. It had been bringing bad luck to me anyways. I wore my socks and went back to bed. Hoping my legs don't toss them out again.

That night I felt something or someone touch my legs. Felt someone removing my socks. Or my legs. I vaguely remembered that because I was so in a deep sleep. I had no idea what happened. Winter sleep!

Next day, I woke up. And didn't see the wind chime on the fan, but the Japanese lady hanging to it from a rope, As if she committed suicide.

I screamed from the inside, but I didn't make any noise. I couldn't. I opened my eyes again. The Japanese lady wasn't hanging from it. It had to be a nightmare.

I couldn't move my legs. It was like my legs were frozen. That was the worst nightmare ever. It apparently gave me Sleep Paralysis. But I only felt that on my legs?

I could see the wind chime near me on the bed. I picked it up. Every time I picked it up I used to see something strange that I never noticed before. And that time I saw the Japanese lady, but with legs, with a smile on her face.

I pushed the covers off of me. Wait. Where were my legs?

I looked down to my bed. The wind chime below me rang.

And where was my fox?

PS: ATLEAST I DIDNT MAKE THE FAN FALL LOL.

GMAIL:

shruti2k5@gmail.com

Printed by Libri Plureos GmbH in Hamburg,
Germany